# MAC CARTHY

## PEOPLE AND PLACES

by

Alicia St Leger

**BALLINAKELLA PRESS**

**1990**

©1990 BALLINAKELLA PRESS
Whitegate, Co. Clare, Ireland.

ISBN 0 946538 26 3

Design: Hugh W. L. Weir
Typesetting and printing: Boethius

## PREFACE AND ACKNOWLEDGEMENTS

The study of a surname can be enlightening both for those who share the surname (or whose ancestors did) and for those interested in the past in general. The MacCarthy story is one which reveals much about the history of Ireland since MacCarthys were involved in many of the major events of the island. The MacCarthy clan held a powerful position in Munster until the late seventeenth century, controlling a large amount of land and many castles. From the eighteenth century onwards the MacCarthys were less important as landowners, but made an important contribution to many fields of endeavour not only in Ireland but in the many countries in which members of the clan settled. It is hoped that this short account of some of the principal MacCarthy people and places will provide information to those interested in the clan and will encourage further research into the history of one of Ireland's most important and colourful families.

Thanks are due to the staff of Cork City Library, particularly Kieran Burke, and the staff of the Boole Library, University College Cork. I am grateful for the encouragement and help given to me during the writing of this book. I would also like to thank Hugh Weir for his encouragement and patience.

*Alicia St Leger*

# CONTENTS

# THE MacCARTHYS OF MUNSTER

The MacCarthy family trace their roots to Ollill Olum, who was King of Munster at the end of the second century A.D. Olill Olum's eldest son was Eoghan Mor, whose descendants included the MacCarthys, O'Sullivans, O'Keeffes and O'Mahonys. These clans held power in the Munster area and were known as the Eoghanacht, because of their descent from Eoghan Mor.

From the fourth century, Cashel in Co. Tipperary became the chief residence of the Eoghanacht kings of Munster. A church was erected there in the fifth century by Aongus, the first Christian King of Munster. Over six hundred years later, King Cormac built an impressive chapel there which was completed in 1134. Until the tenth century, Eoghanacht power was virtually unchallenged in the southern part of Ireland, but this position of strength was increasingly threatened by the growing power of other clans, particularly the Dal Cais from the west (notably Brian Boru) and the O'Neills from the north.

At about this time, the MacCarthy name began to be used. The family is named after Carthach (meaning 'the loving one') King of Munster who was burned to death in 1045 by one of his enemies. Carthach's son Muiredach assumed the name MacCarthach (MacCarthy) meaning 'the son of Carthach.'

Between about 970 and 1170 there was almost constant warfare in Munster as the MacCarthys tried to maintain their power against encroachments by other clans, most notably the O'Briens. In the early twelfth century a settlement was reached which gave the MacCarthys control over south Munster, known as Desmond, while the O'Briens became Kings of Thomond or north Munster.

The struggles between the various groups seeking power in Munster were given a new dimension by the arrival of the Normans in 1169. Diarmaid MacCarthy, King of Desmond, submitted to King Henry II of England in 1171. Diarmaid probably hoped that Henry would protect his territory from the aggressive Norman lords and other rivals, and regarded Henry's authority over the Desmond lands as only nominal. Henry, however, considered himself feudal overlord of the MacCarthy lands and drove Diarmaid out of his eastern territory, dividing it between Milo de Cogan and Robert Fitzstephen. The MacCarthys were pushed to the west and south.

Internal rivalry amongst the MacCarthys weakened their power and aided Norman advancement. This encroachment was halted in the mid-thirteenth century by the successful warfare of Fineen MacCarthy who, in 1261, defeated the Normans at Callan, near Kenmare in Co. Kerry. Following this victory, the MacCarthys retained control in Desmond where they wielded considerable power and influence until the seventeenth century.

The MacCarthys were divided into four main groups from the thirteenth century onwards: (I) The main MacCarthy line was that of the MacCarthy Mor which descended from Domhnall Rua, son of Cormac Fionn (Prince of Desmond 1244-1247). The Duhallow and Muskerry branches of the MacCarthys also descended from Cormac Fionn. The MacCarthy Mor lands extended over Kerry and parts of west Cork, with the principal seat being at Muckross, near Killarney. The power and lands of the clan were frequently challenged by others, both within the clan and from outside. For example, in the early sixteenth century Cormac Ladhrach's position as chief was bitterly disputed by his nephew Tadhg na Lemha. Cormac's son was challenged from outside the clan and had to fight the Fitzmaurices in order to retain his power.

In the mid-sixteenth century the head of the MacCarthy Mor, Domhnall, was generally loyal to the English and sided with them in the Desmond Rebellion. Domhnall was created Earl of Clancare in 1565 and died in 1597. Since he left no legitimate male heir, Clancare's land was divided between the Crown, his natural son and his daughter, Ellen. Ellen inherited most of the MacCarthy Mor land in Kerry and married Florence MacCarthy Reagh, cousin and rival of the chief of that branch of the MacCarthys. Although this land was confiscated during the Cromwellian period, some of it was restored to the descendants of Ellen and Florence MacCarthy in 1663. The Muckross estate eventually passed to the Herbert family in the eighteenth century.

(II) The MacCarthys of Muskerry were a powerful branch and amassed extensive lands in mid-west Cork from the fourteenth century onwards. One of the most notable lords of Muskerry was Cormac Laidir ('the strong') who ruled between 1455 and 1495. Cormac extended his lands eastwards and built several important churches and castles, including Blarney Castle which then became the clan's chief residence. Cormac MacDermod, Lord of Muskerry in the late sixteenth century, fought on the side of the English at the Battle of Kinsale in 1601. Cormac later rebelled, but received a pardon in 1603. His son was created Viscount Muskerry and Lord of Blarney and his grandson, Donogh, fought against Cromwell's armies in the 1650s. Donogh was created Earl of Clancarty by the exiled Charles II and on the Restoration recovered his estates. However, the bulk of the Muskerry lands were again lost to the MacCarthys at the end of the seventeenth century as a result of the Williamite wars.

(III) The MacCarthy Reagh branch held power in the Carbery area of south Cork. This branch was descended from Domhnall Mael Cairprech who defeated the O'Mahonys of East Carbery in the mid-thirteenth century. The name Reagh, meaning 'swarthy', was acquired in the fifteenth century following the victory of the MacCarthy Reagh branch in a succession struggle. The MacCarthy Reagh extended their territory in the fifteenth century and acquired Kilbrittan Castle which became their chief residence. By the early seventeenth century the MacCarthy Reagh were overlords of over five hundred square miles in southwest Cork. The branch lost most of this land through confiscation after the Cromwellian wars of the mid-seventeenth century.

(IV) The MacCarthys of Duhallow, in north west Cork, formed another important branch. The MacCarthys obtained power in the area in the thirteenth century and were based at Kanturk. The Duhallow branch were known as the MacDonogh MacCarthys and were descended from Diarmaid, younger son of Cormac Fionn (Prince of Desmond 1244-1247). Like the MacCarthy Reagh, the Duhallow branch lost their lands and castles in the Cromwellian confiscations.

By the end of the seventeenth century the MacCarthys had lost their pre-eminent position in south Munster and virtually all of their lands and castles were confiscated. Many members of the clan remained in Ireland as tenants, while others settled abroad. The descendants of the Kings of Desmond contributed much to such fields as politics, literature, commerce and religion, not only in Ireland, but also in Britain, France, the United States, Canada, Australia, New Zealand and in many other areas of the world.

## SIGNIFICANT MacCARTHY EVENTS

323 Death of Olill Olum

484 Death of Aongus, first Christian King of Munster

1045 Death of Carthach, King of Munster. His son, Muiredach, assumed name MacCarthach (MacCarthy)

1127 Start of Cormac's Chapel, Cashel (completed 1134) by Cormac MacCarthy, King of Munster

1138 Death of Cormac MacCarthy

1171 Diarmaid MacCarthy, King of Desmond, submitted to King Henry II

1261 Battle of Callan, near Kenmare, Co. Kerry where Fineen MacCarthy defeated the Normans

1295 Kilbrittain Castle captured by the MacCarthys from the de Courceys

1446 Blarney Castle built by Cormac Laidir MacCarthy

1448 Muckross Friary founded by Domhnall MacCarthy Mor

1465 Construction of Kilcrea Castle and Friary by Cormac Laidir MacCarthy

1494 Death of Cormac Laidir MacCarthy

1520 Battle of Mourne Abbey where Cormac Og MacCarthy defeated the Earl of Desmond

1565 Domhnall MacDomhnall MacCarthy created Earl of Clancare

1588 Marriage of Florence MacCarthy Reagh and Ellen MacCarthy Mor

1603 Cormac MacDermot MacCarthy of Blarney pardoned

1609 Work begun on Kanturk Castle by Dermot MacOwen MacDonogh MacCarthy

1616 Death of Cormac MacDermot MacCarthy of Blarney

1628 Cormac Og MacCarthy created Viscount Muskerry and Baron of Blarney

1640 Death of Florence MacCarthy Reagh

| 1658 | Donogh MacCarthy created Earl of Clancarty by (exiled) King Charles II |
|------|----|
| 1685 | Justin MacCarthy received title of Viscount Mountcashel from King James II |
| 1691 | Title of Earl of Clancarty forfeited by Donogh MacCallaghan MacCarthy |
| 1694 | Death of Justin MacCarthy, Viscount Mountcashel |
| 1812 | Sir Charles MacCarthy appointed Governor of Sierra Leone (until 1824) |
| 1817 | Birth of James Joseph McCarthy, architect |
| 1829 | Birth of John George MacCarthy, historian, solicitor, politician |
| 1830 | Birth of Justin McCarthy, journalist, author, politician |
| 1860 | Sir Charles Justin MacCarthy appointed Governor of Ceylon (until 1864) |
| 1874 | John MacCarthy appointed Bishop of Cloyne, Co. Cork. |
| 1882 | Death of Denis Florence MacCarthy, poet |
| 1912 | Death of Justin McCarthy, journalist, author, politician |

# MacCARTHY TITLES OF NOBILITY OR ELECTION

King of Munster
King of Desmond

Prince of Desmond

The MacCarthy Mor
The MacCarthy Reagh

Earl of Clancare
Earl of Clancarty
Count MacCarthy
of Toulouse

Viscount Muskerry
Viscount Mountcashel
Viscount Valentia

Baron of Blarney
Baron of Headington
Baron of Valentia

Lord of Carbery
Lord of Muskerry
Lord of Duhallow

Baronet of Nish,
Co. Armagh

## THE MAC CARTHY ARMS

Most of the leading Irish families are armigorous; that is, they are entitled to bear arms in the form of a decorated shield, often with bearers, and a crest and motto.

Heraldry really developed through the Roman Legions where, in order that he may be identified, the Centurion wore a special sign such as a clenched fist or a dagger on his helmet, different symbols on his shield and had a two part password. The latter was in two parts so that when challenged by the first, a friend would know and pronounce the second which was secret. An enemy would not know this and would be appropriately dealt with. The Romans never invaded Ireland and it was not until the twelfth century Norman conquest that arms were introduced. It was not long before the ancient Irish families including the MacCarthys, adopted the newly introduced symbols. Many adapted tokens, war cries and other symbolism which had been traditional to their Irish past.

Basically, the most used of the MacCarthy arms depict a trippant or trotting stag on their shield. In the case of the MacCarthy More, the heraldic description is "Argent a stag trippant, gules attired and unguled or". This means "a trotting red stag with horns and hooves of gold on a silver background". The most popular crest is "a dexter arm in mail argent, holding in the hand a lizard both propper" which, when displayed, shows a right arm in blue armour from which the normally coloured hand holds a naturally coloured lizard. As regards a Mac Carthy family motto, those used include "Forti et fideli nihil difficile", "Ex arduis perpetuum nomen" and fortes ferox et celer". None, however seems very early. An Irish motto registered to Lieut. Governor of Senegal, Lt. Colonel Charles Mac Carthy in 1812, "Lamh laidir a-buagh" is likely to have been devised from ancient war cries used by other families even though there may have been a genuine but forgotten one genuinely attributable to this important family. The Earl of Clancarty, who was made a count in the seventeenth century, was permitted angels to support his shield but the interpretation of his general arms seems to be lost with time. Nowadays in this commercial age, members of clans bear arms to which they are often not entitled even though they may well be entitled to emblazon themselves with a different shield. Far too often, heraldic artists and purveyors of genealogical information take the easy way out. With the permission of the head of their particular family or of the College of Heraldry in Dublin, members are entitled to their specific arms.

## CORMAC LAIDIR MacCARTHY

14??-1494

Cormac Laidir ('the strong') MacCarthy was ninth Lord of Muskerry between 1455 and 1494 and was one of the most notable leaders of that powerful branch of the MacCarthy clan. He succeeded his father, Tadhg, as chief and during his reign greatly strengthened the power of the MacCarthys of Muskerry.

Cormac Laidir's most important contribution to the authority of the MacCarthys was in the form of the many castles and churches which he built on the eastern boundary of his territory. The most important was Blarney Castle, near Cork city, which he constructed in 1446 and which became the principal seat of the MacCarthys of Muskerry. While Blarney Castle served as the main dwelling place for future MacCarthy chiefs, another of Cormac Laidirs buildings, Kilcrea Friary, served as their main resting place. The Franciscan Abbey at Kilcrea was built in 1465 and had a castle constructed nearby to protect it. Cormac Laidir was buried there in 1494 and it became the burial place of MacCarthy chiefs until the early seventeenth century. Cormac Laidir also built a convent for Augustinian nuns and a castle at Ballymacadane to the south west of Cork City.

As well as constructing buildings, Cormac Laidir increased the areas controlled by his clan and received rent from an area of Cork city and from the western area of Cork harbour. In 1488, by a patent of denization, Cormac Laidir and his successors were given all the rights of Englishmen, thereby securing their loyalty to the Crown.

Carrignamuck Castle, west of the city, was also constructed by Cormac Laidir, probably in the 1450s. It was in this castle that Cormac was fatally wounded by his younger brother Eoghan in 1494. Cormac Laidir was brought to Cork city where he died soon afterwards and was buried near the high alter of Kilcrea Abbey.

13

# CORMAC'S CHAPEL, CASHEL

The magnificent ruins of the Rock of Cashel indicate its importance as a religious and political centre in the past. Cashel was the location of the royal residence of the Kings of Munster from the fourth to the twelfth century. It assumed a religious significance from the mid-fifth century following the conversion of King Aongus to Christianity by St. Patrick. Aongus later erected a church at Cashel, the first of a succession of religious buildings on the site. At the start of the twelfth century, Cashel was presented by King Murtagh O'Brien to the religious of Ireland and after 1110 the Archbishop of Cashel had jurisdiction over the southern half of the country.

One of the most impressive buildings at Cashel is Cormac's Chapel, built between 1127 and 1134. Cormac MacCarthy became King of Munster in 1123 but two years later was ousted by his brother. He spent some time in Lismore, Co. Waterford where he was influenced by the teachings of Bishop Malchus and his pupil St. Malachy. Cormac built two churches at Lismore (which are no longer extant) and in 1127, when he was restored to power at Cashel, he commenced a church there also.

Cormac's Chapel at Cashel is a beautiful Romanesque building, cruciform in design with paired towers and steeply pitched roof. Both interior and exterior are richly embellished with the north door being particularly noteworthy. The success of Cormac's Chapel led to its features being emulated in other church buildings of the period. Cormac MacCarthy died in 1138, but left a fitting monument to his memory on the Rock of Cashel.

The interior of Cormac's Chapel, Cashel

# JUSTIN MacCARTHY, VISCOUNT MOUNTCASHEL

16??-1694

One of the finest MacCarthy military careers was that of Justin MacCarthy, Viscount Mountcashel. Justin was a younger son of the Earl of Clancarty (Donogh MacCarthy of Muskerry) whose power and lands had been largely recovered at the restoration of King Charles II in 1660. The family fared well under Charles II and his brother James II, but the overthrow of the latter also led to a demise in the MacCarthy fortunes.

Justin MacCarthy's career was closely linked to that of King James II. In 1685 when James ordered that regiments be placed under Roman Catholic officers, Justin MacCarthy was one of the first officers to be given such a command. He served loyally in James' army and in 1689 the king bestowed on him the title of Viscount Mountcashel.

Justin .MacCarthy was one of King James' most important military officers during the Williamite wars, but was defeated and taken prisoner in July 1689 by the Enniskilleners at Newtownbutler, Co. Fermanagh. Fortunately for Mountcashel, he managed to escape from his captors and in 1690 went to France where he commanded Irish regiments in the service of King Louis XIV. The Irish forces were sent to France in exchange for the military assistance which Louis XIV had given to James in March 1690 when over 6,003 soldiers under the Comte de Lauzun arrived in Ireland. In exchange, Mountcashel led over 5,000 Irish soldiers in campaigns against adversaries of the French in Savoy, Catalonia and Germany. Mountcashel's Irish regiments proved to be excellent soldiers and impressed the French military leaders. After the final defeat of James' cause, many other Irish soldiers joined Louis' armies on the continent.

Justin MacCarthy, Lord Viscount Mountcashel

Mountcashel soon established a reputation as a fine military leader and fought well in the campaigns in France, Spain and Germany. He suffered an injury early in his career in France which never fully healed and which affected his health. In 1694 Mountcashel visited the baths at Barege hoping to improve his condition, but his health declined and he died there on 1st of July 1894.

KILBRITTAIN CASTLE. Adam.

# KILBRITTAIN CASTLE

The site of Kilbrittain Castle, between Kinsale and Timoleague in west Cork, was closely linked to the MacCarthy family from the thirteenth to the seventeenth centuries. The MacCarthys asserted their power there in the thirteenth century by defeating the O'Mahonys, but were strongly challenged for control of the area by the Norman de Cogans and de Courceys.

By the late thirteenth century the de Courceys had constructed a castle at Kilbrittain which was seized by the MacCarthys in 1295. The MacCarthys held the castle until 1430 but lost it to the de Courceys for several periods over the following century. This rivalry continued until 1510 when the MacCarthys finally regained control of the castle which they held until the Cromwellian wars. Kilbrittain was the main stronghold of the MacCarthy Reagh branch of the MacCarthy clan which held considerable power in the Carbery area of south Cork.

There is a story told that when the MacCarthys regained the castle in 1510, it was because the de Courceys failed to keep their side of a bargain. The de Courceys had borrowed a ferret from the MacCarthys who demanded that Kilbrittain Castle would be security for its safe return. The ferret died and the MacCarthys returned to the castle'

The 1537 rebellion of 'Silken Thomas' Fitzgerald, a member of the family of the powerful Earls of Kildare, had an impact on Kilbrittain Castle. The widow of Daniel MacCarthy Reagh (who died in 1531) was a Fitzgerald and she secretly sheltered the young Kildare heir, Gerald, in the castle for a time.

The MacCarthy Reagh continued to occupy the castle until the bitter warfare of the Cromwellian period. Cormac MacCarthy Reagh was absent from Kilbrittain Castle in June 1642 when a Parliamentary army forced the surrender of the fortress. Cormac never regained the castle and lands which were lost to the MacCarthy family from that period.

The castle was initially given to the Cromwellian Colonel Thomas Long and later passed through several owners until it was purchased by Jonas Stawell in 1690. It remained in that family until the early twentieth century and was substantially modified in mid-eighteenth and mid-nineteenth century alterations. The castle was burnt in 1920 during the War of Independence, but has since been reconstructed and retains an air of grandeur appropriate to the site of one of the main strongholds of the MacCarthy Reagh.

## FLORENCE MacCARTHY REAGH

c.1562-c.1640

Florence MacCarthy Reagh was born about 1652 and was the eldest son of Sir Donnchadh, chief of the MacCarthy Reagh from 1566 to 1576. Florence grew up in the Carbery area of south-east Cork where he received a good education, learning English, Latin and Spanish as well as studying the law. He fought on the side of the English during the Desmond Rebellion and afterwards was rewarded by Queen Elizabeth I.

Florence's good relations with the Crown came to an end in 1588 when he married Ellen MacCarthy Mor, the daughter and only legitimate heir of the Earl of Clancare (the MacCarthy Mor). The English had planned for Ellen to marry an English nobleman, such as the son of Sir Valentine Browne who was an important English landowner in Kerry. By their marriage Florence and Ellen not only destroyed these plans,but they also united two of the most powerful families in Munster. This was directly contrary to the Elizabethan policy of weakening and dividing the powerful Irish clans in order to assert her Royal power.

Florence's marriage led to his arrest and incarceration in the Tower of London by early 1589. He remained there for nearly two years when he was liberated on condition that he did not leave London without permission. In 1593 he was allowed to return to Ireland. The growing discontent of the powerful O'Neill and O'Donnell clans in Ireland led the Crown to try to ensure Florence's loyalty by confirming his land to him and dropping all charges against him. Florence apparently tried to keep on good terms with both the Crown and the rebel forces under O'Neill and O'Donnell. He communicated with the latter and received the title of MacCarthy Mor from them, claiming the title through his marriage to Ellen. These actions were regarded with suspicion by the Crown and in 1601 Florence was again arrested. He spent the rest of his life either in prison or under confinement or restriction of some sort. During this period from 1601 until his death in about 1640, Florence was occupied with petitions for his release and with law suits about his property. He also wrote a treatise on the early history of Ireland and preserved important old annals of Ireland. Florence MacCarthy Reagh was one of the most colourful members of that branch of the MacCarthy family.

Carrignamuck Castle
(see Cormac Laidir MacCarthy, p. 13)

# MUCKROSS FRIARY

The Muckross area near Killarney in Co. Kerry was the principal seat of the main MacCarthy line, the MacCarthy Mor. In 1448 Domhnall MacCarthy Mor founded a Franciscan Friary there, which is now usually referred to as Muckross Abbey. The Friary was constructed on the site of an earlier church and took fifty years to complete. For about two centuries the Franciscan community lived at Muckross before being finally dispersed in the mid-seventeenth century.

In 1588 the Friary played a central role in the affairs of the MacCarthy clan, for it was there that Ellen, daughter and heir of the MacCarthy Mor (the Earl of Clancare) married Florence MacCarthy Reagh. This wedding was completely against the wished of the Crown authorities which had hoped to see Ellen married to a loyal English nobleman. Thus, the wedding took place amidst great secrecy and the ceremony is reputed to have been held at midnight. Eight years later Ellen's father, the Earl of Clancare, died and was interred in the choir of the Friary.

The impact of the Reformation and the unsettled state of the area led to disruptions at Muckross Friary from the late sixteenth century onwards. In the early seventeenth century, following several absences from the building, the friars returned and altered sections of the Friary. They fled for a time after 1630, but were again in occupation of the building when it was taken over by Cromwell's forces in 1652. The Friary was not occupied after the mid-seventeenth century, but the MacCarthys retained their Muckross property until the late eighteenth century when the last MacCarthy Mor died. The Muckross estates were then willed to the Herbert family.

The remains of the Friary can still be seen on the Muckross estate which is now part of a national park. A yew tree grows in the

The Choir of Muckross Abbey

centre of the cloister and it is said that it is fatal to cut or harm the tree in any way! The tower and windows are particularly attractive remnants of this important MacCarthy foundation.

# COUNT JUSTIN MacCARTHY

1744-1812

Members of the MacCarthy family were renowned not only in their own country, but also in foreign lands. Justin MacCarthy, who was born in Ireland in 1744, became a respected member of the French court and established an important branch of the MacCarthy family in the Toulouse area of France.

Justin MacCarthy belonged to the MacCarthy Reagh branch of the MacCarthy clan. He grew up at Spring House, Co. Tipperary where his great grandfather had settled in the mid-seventeenth century. The restrictions of the Penal Laws in Ireland led to the emigration of Justin's father, Denis, who eventually settled in France. Justin soon followed suit, sold his Irish property and established himself in Toulouse. There he and his wife raised their children, the most notable of whom was Abbé Nicholas Tuite MacCarthy who was a renowned preacher.

In 1776 Justin MacCarthy was naturalised as a French subject. He was also given the title of Count and granted the privileges of the French court by King Louis XVI. He was a noted scholar and linguist and soon had a fine collection of art and literature assembled in his house. His library was said to rival that of the King of France. It contained rare and beautifully bound books and was greatly admired and valued. The Duke of Devonshire offered £25,000 for MacCarthy's collection after the latter's death, but the hostile relations between England and France meant that the transaction was not possible. MacCarthy's library was sold in France for about £16,500 and the important collection of books was dispersed. While the Count's library was his most prized and admired possession, he also collected important art works and paintings. Unfortunately, these were also dispersed after his death.

Count MacCarthy died in Toulouse in 1812, but the family name continued there until the early twentieth century. His descendants were known as the MacCarthy Levignac, named for a Bordeaux property belonging to the Count. Justin MacCarthy was a scholarly and well-respected gentleman and was a worthy representative of the MacCarthy family in France.

Blarney Castle

# BLARNEY CASTLE

One of the best known Irish castles is that of the MacCarthy fortification at Blarney, near Cork city. Blarney Castle was built in 1446 by Cormac Laidir MacCarthy and was later expanded at the end of the fifteenth century. It became the principal seat of the powerful MacCarthys of Muskerry and remained in MacCarthy hands for over two hundred years.

Blarney Castle was built by Cormac Laidir MacCarthy in order to safeguard his lands. His descendant Sir Cormac MacTeige MacCarthy had the same aim in mind when he obtained his land by royal patent in 1578, thus confirming his personal ownership of the property. His nephew, Cormac MacDermot, succeeded to most of his property and also the title Lord of Muskerry. Cormac MacDermot MacCarthy was one of the most colourful of the chiefs of the MacCarthys of Muskerry. His claims to Cormac MacTeige's property was disputed by the latter's son, Cormac Og. In order to secure his claim, Cormac MacDermot surrendered his property to the Crown and obtained a re-grant in 1596. In doing this he cleverly out-manoeuvred Cormac Og, but was not free of subsequent challenges by his cousin and his adherents.

Cormac MacDermot also had to deal with the power of the Crown which was suspicious of his loyalty during the difficult political and military upheavals of the period. In 1595 Cormac MacDermot's forces at Blarney Castle foiled an attempt by the English military leader, George Carew, to seize Blarney by subterfuge. Carew had hoped that a number of his men could enter the castle under the guise of needing refreshment after a deer hunting expedition. They were granted refreshment but outside the castle walls!

Cormac MacDermot MacCarthy gave some rather reluctant support to the English at the Battle of Kinsale in 1601, but his loyalty was suspected by the Crown. Shortly afterwards he was arrested, but subsequently escaped and joined his cousin, Donal O'Sullivan Beare, in rebellion. He later submitted to the Crown and received a pardon in 1603.

Cormac MacDermot showed considerable skill in maintaining his power against challenges from his clan, the Crown and others. His ability to keep on good terms with several sides at one time,without committing himself, earned him a reputation for clever diplomacy. His flattery and persuasive conversation is reputed to have led Queen Elizabeth I to refer to him as being "all blarney". The art of flattering conversation later became linked with a particular stone in Blarney Castle and gave rise to the belief that eloquence was conferred on those who kissed the stone.

Cormac MacDermot's son and successor, Cormac Og, was conferred with the titles of Viscount Muskerry and Baron of Blarney. His successor, Donogh, was one of the main Confederate leaders in Munster during the Cromwellian wars, until his surrender in 1652. He later went to France where he was created Earl of Clancarty by the exiled King Charles II in 1658. This loyalty to the Royal cause resulted in most of Clancarty's lands being returned to him in 1662, after the Restoration.

Blarney did not remain for long in MacCarthy hands. The fourth Earl of Clancarty, Donogh, joined the forces of James II in the Williamite wars. The 1690 defeat of James resulted in the loss of virtually all of the MacCarthy lands, including Blarney Castle.

The Castle passed through several owners before being sold to Sir James Jeffreys in the early eighteenth century. It eventually descended to the Colthurst family who still live on the estate. Blarney Castle is now a popular place for visitors who can admire the magnificent structure which was once the chief castle of the noble MacCarthys of Muskerry.

# JOHN GEORGE MacCARTHY

1829-1892

John MacCarthy was born in Cork in 1829 and in his lifetime made an important contribution to the legal, historical and cultural development of his native country. When only twenty years of age, MacCarthy founded the Cork Historical Society in association with his namesake, Justin MacCarthy. John MacCarthy retained a strong interest in history throughout his life and in 1856 published a lecture on the history of Cork. MacCarthy's short history proved popular and had been issued in a third edition by 1870. He also was the author of "The French Revolution of 1792; its causes etc." (1884) and of a monograph on Henry Grattan which was published in 1886.

While historical matters were of continuing interest to John MacCarthy, his professional career revolved around the law and politics. From 1853 to 1881 he practiced as a solicitor in Cork and between 1874 and 1880 represented Mallow as a Member of Parliament. This background resulted in his close involvement with the implementation of the various Land Acts which were passed by Parliament in the late nineteenth century. MacCarthy acted as Assistant Court Commissioner under the 1881 Land Act, a position he held for five years. He was then made Court Commissioner under the 1885 Land Act, and held that position until his death in 1892. His skill at dealing with the often difficult land problem was based on a detailed study of the question. In 1870 he had published a pamphlet on the Irish land question, while in 1875 he wrote "The Farmer's Guide to the Land Act."

As well as his professional interests, John MacCarthy was closely involved with the Cork Young Men's Society which he founded in 1852 and of which he was President until 1880. MacCarthy was made a Knight of the Order of St. Gregory by Pope Leo XIII in 1880.

John George MacCarthy

This successful and talented man died in London in 1892 at the age of sixty three and was buried in Glasnevin Cemetery in Dublin.

# CARRIGNAVAR CASTLE

The MacCarthys of Carrignavar represented an important branch of the MacCarthys of Muskerry. Cormac MacDermot of Blarney Castle died in 1617 and left two sons, Cormac (later Viscount Muskerry) and Donal. Donal had a castle built at Carrignavar probably in the early seventeenth century and his descendants lived in the castle and later in the nearby house, until the early twentieth century.

Carrignavar House

Carrignavar Castle was one of the last castles held by the MacCarthys of Muskerry to be captured by Cromwell's forces in 1650. The property was recovered ten years later by Donogh MacCarthy, Earl of Clancarty, who leased it back to his relations, the MacCarthys of Carrignavar. The castle was one of the few MacCarthy properties to remain in their hands following the upheavals of the Williamite wars in the late seventeenth century. During that period, the Penal Laws were enacted thereby restricting the rights of Roman Catholic property owners, especially with regard to inheritance. Charles MacCarthy initially gave Carrignavar in trust to a Protestant friend, but, concerned at the vulnerability of the property, he later converted to Protestantism and thus secured the estate for his descendants.

In the eighteenth century Carrignavar Castle became an important centre for the survival of traditional Gaelic forms of literature and music. Unfortunately there are few remains of this important MacCarthy castle.

Carrignavar House was constructed in the late nineteenth century to the south-east of the castle and was inhabited by the MacCarthy family until the early twentieth century. It is a fine castellated house and is attractively situated near the ruins of the old castle. By the 1940s the long MacCarthy association with Carrignavar had been broken when the property was sold to the Sheedy family and subsequently passed to the Sacred Heart Fathers.

# JUSTIN McCARTHY

1830-1912

Justin MacCarthy, October 1886

Justin McCarthy was born near Cork on November 22nd 1830.
Since his family could not afford to educate him in law, the young
Justin turned to journalism instead. His first job was with the
Cork Examiner which he joined in 1848. Six years later he moved
to Liverpool and wrote for the Northern Daily Times until 1859.

He then moved again, this time to London where the Morning Star offered employment for his journalistic talents. From 1864 to 1868 McCarthy was editor of the Star and from 1870 was leader writer on the Daily News.

McCarthy's writing abilities were not confined to newspaper journalism and he became well known for his historical and biographical work and his novels. His five volume "History of Our Own Times", published between 1879 and 1897, was his best known historical work, while his other successes included the novel "Dear Lady Disdain" (1875) and his two volume "Reminiscences" (1899).

As well as being a talented and successful writer, Justin McCarthy was active in the political life of his country. From 1871 he played an important role in the Irish Parliamentary Party which sought Home Rule for Ireland. McCarthy was Member of Parliament for Longford between 1879 and 1886 and then represented Derry City from 1886 to 1892. In 1890 the party's fortunes received a serious blow when its popular leader, Charles Stewart Parnell, faced political ruin following a divorce case. The party split between the majority who felt that Parnell should resign in the interests of the Home Rule cause, and those who remained committed to their leader. Justin McCarthy supported the former group and as Chairman of the Irish Parliamentary Party from 1890 to 1896 was one of the main anti-Parnellite leaders in the period.

By the late 1890s McCarthy's declining health and failing eyesight forced him to withdraw from politics. Thereafter he occupied himself with his literary works, his near blindness necessitating the dictation of his reminiscences and novels. From 1903 he received £300 per annum from a civil list pension granted to him for his services to literature. Justin McCarthy died at Folkestone, Kent on 24th April 1912.

## KILCREA CASTLE AND FRIARY

Cormac Laidir MacCarthy, renowned for the castle which he constructed at Blarney, was also the builder of Kilcrea Castle and Friary. Both were erected about 1465 near the banks of the River Bride to the west of Cork city.

The Friary was built for the Franciscans who remained there until the early seventeenth century. Kilcrea Friary had special significance

Kilcrea Friary, from an old print

as a burial place of the chiefs of the MacCarthys of Muskerry. Amongst those interred there were Cormac Laidir MacCarthy (who built the Friary) and his son Cormac Og who defeated the Earl of Desmond in an important battle at Mourne Abbey in 1520. Also buried there was Cormac MacDermot MacCarthy of Blarney Castle whose eloquence was reputedly referred to as "all blarney". Monks no longer inhabited Kilcrea Friary after the early seventeenth century, but members of the MacCarthy clan were interred there for the next two hundred years. The Friary itself was taken over by the Cromwellian Captain John Bailey in the 1640s.

Kilcrea Castle was inhabited by Sir Cormac MacDermot MacCarthy until 1589 when he moved to Blarney Castle. On his arrest Kilcrea Castle was surrendered to Crown forces, but was subsequently returned to him. It remained in MacCarthy hands until the Cromwellian wars when it was confiscated and granted to Admiral William Penn. The Restoration of the monarchy in 1660 saw Donogh MacCarthy, Earl of Clancarty, regain the castle and lands. However, the upheavals of the Williamite period resulted in the confiscation of the Kilcrea property which subsequently passed into the hands of the Hedges family. The ruins of this important MacCarthy castle and friary attest to the significance of that clan in the history of the area.

Armagh Cathedral, completed by J. J. McCarthy

# JAMES JOSEPH McCARTHY

1817-1882

One of the most prolific church architects of mid-nineteenth century Ireland was James Joseph McCarthy. McCarthy was involved in the design of about eighty buildings all over Ireland, the vast majority of which were Roman Catholic churches.

McCarthy was born in Dublin in 1817 to a family which had Kerry connections. His upbringing was constrained by the humble circumstances of his family, but he received a good education and trained as an architect in Dublin. Having spent some time in England, McCarthy returned to Ireland about 1846 and from then until his death in 1882 he was closely involved with ecclesiastical architecture in Ireland.

McCarthy was strongly influenced by the work of A. W. N. Pugin whose ideas on Gothic architecture he greatly admired. The majority of McCarthys churches were designed in Gothic style, a style which became very popular in mid-century for the large number of Roman Catholic churches erected during that period. McCarthy favoured Decorated Gothic, but also used Early English Gothic and for a few of his designs employed the Romanesque style. His close involvement with church planning was reflected in his activity in the Irish Ecclesiological Society and his writings on religious architecture.

McCarthy was fortunate in practising at a time of revival for the Roman Catholic church following Emancipation in 1829. Growing confidence in the church was reflected in the spate of church building during the nineteenth century. At the same time there was growing national consciousness within the Roman Catholic church and a desire to reflect the past history of Ireland in its designs. McCarthy, as an Irish Catholic nationalist, was an architect in whom the Roman Catholic church could have confidence and whose designs reflected the general preferences of the church. McCarthy's support for the Young Ireland movement of the 1840s and his friendship with Charles Gavan Duffy revealed his nationalist beliefs.

J. J. McCarthy was an able administrator and was generally successful in carrying out church designs which reflected the preferences and means of the parishes involved. He designed a large number of churches for both city and country locations. Amongst his rural commissions were:St. Kevin's Church, Glendalough, Co. Wicklow; St. Mary's Church, Dingle, Co. Kerry; and the parish church at Clogheen, Co. Tipperary. McCarthy's city churches included St. Saviour's, Dominick Street, Dublin and St. Catherine's, Meath Street, Dublin. Four Roman Catholic cathedrals were also built to designs of McCarthy. St. Patrick's Cathedral, Armagh and St. Eugene's Cathedral, Derry were completed to McCarthy's plans, while he was solely responsible for the Cathedral of St. Macartan, Monaghan and the Romanesque Cathedral at Thurles, Co. Tipperary. McCarthy also designed the chapel at St. Patrick's College, Maynooth and one of his few secular creations was the Venetian style Cahirmoyle House, Co. Limerick.

McCarthy's son, Charles J., was also an architect and assisted his father's work during the last years of the latter's life. J. J. McCarthy died in Dublin in 1882, but the churches which he designed are a proud reminder of his life's work.

## MACROOM CASTLE

Macroom Castle was one of the main castles of the MacCarthys of Muskerry and had a particularly colourful history. The De Cogans probably built the original castle which was burned at the end of the thirteenth century by Fineen MacCarthy. His descendant Cormac MacCarthy was granted the castle and lands at Macroom in the early fourteenth century as a reward for defeating his rebellious nephew. Cormac's son, Dermot Mor, established himself in Muskerry where the family soon assumed a pre-eminent position.

Macroom Castle

Macroom Castle underwent renovations in the sixteenth century, but in 1602 was destroyed by fire. In that year the English forces were attempting to subdue the country after the upheavals surrounding the Battle of Kinsale. Cormac MacDermot

MacCarthy,who owned Macroom Castle, was imprisoned in Cork and the Castle was besieged by Crown forces. Unfortunately for the defenders, just as the English army was about to depart, a fire accidently started within the castle forcing the garrison to abandon the building to their enemies. Cormac MacDermot was subsequently pardoned in 1603 and he repaired the castle.

The Cromwellian period led to more drama for the castle. In 1642 Cardinal Rinnuccini stayed in the building en route to the Confederation of Kilkenny. Six years later an army was assembled at Macroom to attack the Parliamentary forces at Clonmel. The army, led by Bishop Boethius MacEgan, was attacked and defeated by Colonel Broghill outside Macroom Castle. The Castle was burned by the garrison who joined MacEgan's army. The property was later granted to Admiral William Penn who was the father of the founder of the state of Pennsylvania in the United States. The castle was again burned about 1650.

The Restoration of King Charles II led to the MacCarthys regaining their property at Macroom, Penn being given other land as compensation. Donogh MacCarthy, Earl of Clancarty, rebuilt the castle but the family did not enjoy their property for long. The wars of the late seventeenth century saw Macroom Castle held by Williamite forces and both castle and lands were confiscated from the MacCarthys once that conflict was over.

Macroom Castle eventually belonged to the Hedges-Eyre family and passed through inheritance to the Earls of Bantry and to Lord Ardilaun. In 1922 it suffered a fate common in its history when it was burnt during the Irish Civil War. The shell of this historic castle is now part of a public park.

# DENIS FLORENCE MacCARTHY

1817-1882

Denis Florence MacCarthy was amongst the more prominent poets in Ireland during the nineteenth century. His own poetic and prose compositions and his translations of other writers were much admired both in Ireland and abroad.

MacCarthy was born in Dublin in 1817 and was educated at Trinity College Dublin and at Maynooth. He showed promise as a writer from an early age and had published poetry by the time he was seventeen. He was active in the political movements of the period and supported the Repeal movement which sought Catholic Emancipation. MacCarthy later joined the Young Ireland movement and contributed political verse to the Nation and other publications.

Denis MacCarthy was perhaps best known for his translations of the Spanish writer Calderon. Between 1848 and 1873 he produced six volumes of Calderon's translated works, an accomplishment for which he received much praise. In 1881 he was awarded a medal by the Royal Academy of Spain in recognition of his achievement.

MacCarthy was a talented writer and published several volumes of his own work. In 1846 he produced "The Poets and Dramatists of Ireland" and four years later published "Ballads, Poems and Lyrics". In 1882, the year of his death, another volume of his poetry appeared. Amongst his other works were centenary odes on Daniel O'Connell and Thomas Moore. MacCarthy lived in London for about ten years from 1872 and in his first year there published a work on the early life of the great English poet, Percy Shelley.

MacCarthy's contributions to literature were recognised by his being granted a civil list pension of £100 in 1870. Denis MacCarthy returned to Ireland near the end of his life and died in Blackrock, Co. Dublin, in 1882.

# KANTURK CASTLE

The MacCarthys rose to power in north-west Cork in the thirteenth century and remained important for over four hundred years. Those of Duhallow, known as the MacDonogh MacCarthys, had their chief fortification at Kanturk.

The original Kanturk Castle was plundered in 1510 by the Earl of Kildare and the present building was constructed on a different site, about a mile from Kanturk. Work was begun about 1609 by Dermot MacOwen MacDonogh MacCarthy, who had seized the lordship of Duhallow in 1585 against the claims of both his cousin, Donogh MacCormac, and later of Donogh's son. As well as dealing with this internal clan rivalry, Dermot MacOwen also showed determination in his relations with outside forces. His denunciation of Queen Elizabeth and the danger he posed to Crown authority during the revolt of O'Neill and O'Donnell, led to his imprisonment in 1601. Dermot MacOwen was released in 1604, but continued to be regarded with suspicion by the Crown until his death in about 1620.

Dermot MacOwen's castle, which was a fortified court rather than a traditional tower house, was never completed and stands as a roofless shell. Legends grew up about its construction, including tales of cruelty to the workers who built it and a prophesy that it would never be inhabited. It is suggested that the Crown authorities halted its progress because of Dermot MacOwen's suspect loyalty, but it is more likely that he simply could not afford to finish it. His estates were heavily mortgaged to Sir Philip Perceval whose descendants successfully claimed the property after its confiscation during the Cromwellian period. The Perceval family, later Earls of Egmont, owned Kanturk Castle until 1889 when it was transferred to the Society for the Preservation of National Monuments. It is still maintained by the Office of Public Works and is a monument to the ambitions of Dermot MacOwen MacDonogh MacCarthy.

Kanturk Castle

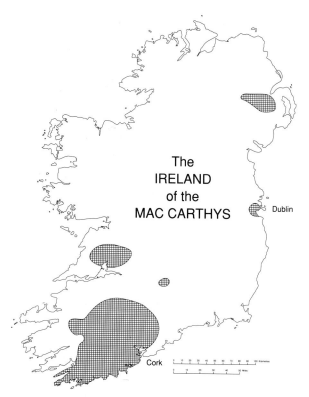

Ireland. Main MacCarthy Areas.

## BOOK OF LISMORE

The Book of Lismore is more accurately described as the Book of MacCarthy Reagh. It is a large volume of writings composed of theological, historical and romantic literature. This work was compiled on the occasion of the marriage of Finghin MacCarthy Reagh and Catherine, daughter of Thomas, Earl of Desmond, at the end of the fifteenth century. The book remained in the family castle of Kilbrittain until 1642 when the building was captured by English forces led by the Earl of Cork's son. The book was removed from the castle and taken to the seat of the Earl of Cork at Lismore Castle, Co. Waterford, where it was discovered in 1814.

## McCARTHY CUP

The McCarthy Cup is presented each year to the All-Ireland Senior Hurling Champions. It is named after Liam McCarthy who presented the trophy for the first time in the 1921 final, when it was won by Limerick. McCarthy was born in Ballygarvan near Cork and emigrated to London where he was closely involved in the promotion of Gaelic games. He was the first president of the Provincial Council of Britain and kept up a keen interest in all aspects of Gaelic sport until his death in 1928.

## McCARTHY MONUMENT

A tall decorated column, standing twenty-five feet high, is located on the Blackrock Road, Cork, as a monument to the MacCarthy clan. Alexander McCarthy, Member of Parliament for Cork in 1860, was responsible for its erection in the late nineteenth century. It was designed by W. B. Atkins and has carvings depicting MacCarthy people and events.

## MacCARTHY "MASTERS"

The vast MacCarthy clan was divided into many sub-groups, some of whom became closely identified with certain areas. Teige MacCarthy was granted the Abbey and Castle of Mourne, Co. Cork, in 1542 and his successors were known as the "Masters of Mourne". Other MacCarthy "Masters" were the "Masters of Mona" who lived at Courtbrack Castle near Blarney and who were descended from Donogh MacCarthy na Mona. Both these titles were in use until the end of the eighteenth century.

# SOME MacCARTHY PLACES

### BALLEA CASTLE

Ballea Castle, which is still occupied as a private residence, was built by the MacCarthys of Cloghroe in the sixteenth century near Carrigaline, Co. Cork. The MacCarthy family remained in the castle until 1690, although they were ousted for a time during the Cromwellian period. The property then passed to the Hodder family who lived in the castle until the early twentieth century.

### BALLINOROHER CASTLE

Situated near the west Cork village of Timoleague, Ballinoroher Castle was built by a branch of the MacCarthy Reagh of Carbery. It was probably constructed in the early seventeenth century and is still in good condition.

### BALLYCARBERY CASTLE

One of the most westerly strongholds of the MacCarthys was Ballycarbery Castle near Valentia, Co. Kerry. It was probably built by the MacCarthys in the fifteenth or sixteenth centuries and was inhabited by the O'Connells who acted as constables to the powerful MacCarthy Mor clan.

### BALLYMACADANE CASTLE

Ballymacadane Castle, near Ballincollig, Co. Cork, was one of the many buildings attributed to Cormac Laidir MacCarthy. It was constructed in the mid-15th century with the aim of protecting a nearby Augustinian convent. No remains of this fortress now exist.

### BALLYVODANE CASTLE

There is only a fragment left of this MacCarthy castle near Blarney

The
IRELAND
of the
MAC CARTHYS

Belfast •

• Dublin

• Ennis

• Cashel

• Kanturk

Killarney
• Muckross

Blarney
•

Cork
•

Macroom •

Kilcrea
•

Kilbrittain
Timoleague • •

| 0 | 10 | 20 | 30 | 40 | 50 | 60 | 70 | 80 | 90 | 100 Kilometres |

| 0 | 10 | 20 | 30 | 40 | 50 Miles |

Ireland. Significant MacCarthy Places

47

in Co. Cork. It once belonged to the MacCarthys of Muskerry, but appears to have been derelict by the mid-seventeenth century.

## BENDUFF CASTLE

This MacCarthy castle, near Rosscarbery in west Cork, now forms part of a guesthouse. It was built about 1470 and by the seventeenth century it belonged to the MacCarthy Reagh clan. The MacCarthys held the castle until 1642 when it was granted to the Cromwellian Major Apollo Morris. The MacCarthys never regained possession of the castle, which was enlarged in the later seventeenth century.

## BLARNEY CASTLE (See page 27)

## CAHIRMOYLE HOUSE

This beautiful Victorian house in Ardagh, Co. Limerick was designed by J.J. McCarthy, a well known nineteenth century Irish architect. Most of McCarthy's designs were for churches, but this Celtic-Romanesque style dwelling is one of his few secular works. He made attractive use of pink and grey stone in its design. Cahirmoyle was built in 1871 and now belongs to a religious order.

## CARRAIG DERMOT OGE

This castle, as its name suggests, was built by Dermot Oge MacCarthy in the late fifteenth century. Dermot Oge was the nephew of a well known castle builder - Cormac Laidir MacCarthy. The castle, located near Macroom, Co. Cork, was occupied by the MacCarthys and later by the MacSwineys who were professional soldiers. Unfortunately, there are few remains left of Carraig Dermot Oge.

## CARRICKAPHOOCA CASTLE

The tall tower of this MacCarthy castle still stands as a reminder of the power of the MacCarthys in the Macroom area of Co. Cork.

APPROXIMATE BARONY
DIVISIONS - CORK & KERRY.

Clare

Limerick

Tipperary

Waterford

CORK

KERRY

IRAGHT
O'Connor

Clanmaurice

Trughanacmy

Corkaguiny

Iveragh

Dunkerron

Magunihy

Duhallow

Orrery

Fermoy

Gibbon

Barrymore

Barretts

Cork

(Cork)

Kerrycurrihy

Kinsale

Courceys

East
Muskery

West
Muskery

Kinal
meaky

Kinalea

East
Carbery

Ibane

Glenarought

Bear

Bantry

West
Carbery

49

Carrickaphooca was built about 1436 by Dermot Mor MacCarthy, a brother of Cormac Laidir MacCarthy. In the late sixteenth century a family dispute led to the castle being attacked and the garrison was forced to surrender. It was later restored to the MacCarthys of Drishane and remained in MacCarthy hands until 1690 when it was lost in the Williamite confiscations.

## CARRIGADROHID CASTLE

This castle was constructed about 1455 by Cormac MacCarthy and is situated near Macroom, Co. Cork. In 1650 it was the scene of a siege when Bishop Boethtius MacEgan of Ross was brought by the Cromwellians to urge the garrison to surrender. When MacEgan instead encouraged them to fight, he was hanged outside the walls of the fortress. The castle later surrendered. Carrigadrohid was held by the MacCarthys until 1703 and eventually passed to the Bowen family. Its outer walls still remain.

## CARRIGNAMUCK CASTLE

The great builder, Cormac Laidir MacCarthy, was responsible for the erection of this fine castle which still stands near Dripsey, Co. Cork. It was while he was in Carrignamuck that Cormac Laidir was murdered in 1494 by his brother and sons. The castle later became the usual residence of the tanist (probable successor) of the MacCarthys of Muskerry. It was attacked during the Cromwellian period, was lost to the MacCarthys after 1690 and eventually became the property of the Bowen-Colthursts who restored it in 1866.

## CARRIGNAVAR CASTLE AND HOUSE (See page 31)

## CASTLE FORBES

This castle-style house was built about 1830 in Newtownforbes, Co. Longford. In the 1870s additions to the house were designed by the architect J. J. McCarthy.

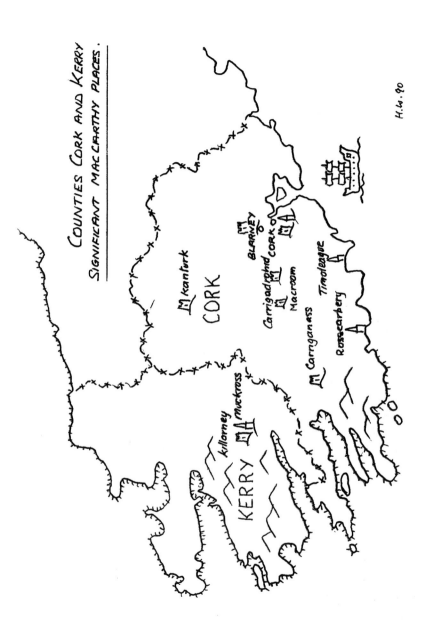

COUNTIES CORK AND KERRY
SIGNIFICANT MACCARTHY PLACES.

H.W. 90

CORK

Kanturk

Blarney

Carrigadrohid
CORK
Macroom

Timoleague

Carriganass

Rosscarbery

KERRY

Killarney
Muckross

51

## CASTLE INCH

This castle was the subject of dispute between two powerful families in the Inniscarra area of Co. Cork: the (Norman) Barretts and the MacCarthys of Muskerry. It was built by the Barretts but by the sixteenth century belonged to the MacCarthys. In 1588 it was regranted to the Barretts, but the wily Cormac MacDermot MacCarthy of Blarney eventually succeeded in having it restored to him by 1600. Castle Inch was confiscated by Cromwell but regained by the MacCarthys under King Charles II. It was occupied for a time by the noted soldier, Justin MacCarthy, Viscount Mountcashel. It was lost to the MacCarthys after 1690 and was in ruins by 1750. The site of this castle is now under water, being part of the Inniscarra dam.

## CASTLELOUGH

This castle was beautifully situated beside one of the lakes of Killarney in Co. Kerry. Castlelough was once owned by the MacCarthy Mor and in the late sixteenth century the castle was mortgaged by the Earl of Clancare to his son-in-law Florence MacCarthy Reagh. Although confiscated during the Cromwellian era, the castle was restored to the MacCarthys in 1663 and was one of the few MacCarthy properties to remain in the family after 1690. In 1745 it was sold to Col. William Crosbie. There are only a few remains left of this MacCarthy Mor castle.

## CASTLEMORE

The curtain wall and towers remain of this fortress which was constructed in the late fifteenth century at Crookstown, Co. Cork. It was one of the most important MacCarthy castles and was occupied by the MacCarthys themselves until the late sixteenth century and thereafter by their soldiers, the MacSwineys. The MacCarthys lost the castle during the Cromwellian wars and did not regain it. It was occupied until the mid-eighteenth century.

## CHATEAU DE LA BROSSE

The beautiful Chateau de la Brosse is situated in north central France and is inhabited by the descendants of MacCarthys who fled from Ireland after the collapse of the Jacobite cause in 1690. A member of the Clan Diarmud branch of the MacCarthy Reagh eventually settled in France and his descendants acquired the Chateau in the late nineteenth century.

## CHATEAU DE ST-GERY

This French chateau is located about twenty four miles north of Toulouse. It was linked to the MacCarthy family from the early nineteenth century when the Marquis de St-Gery married Marie Christine de MacCarthy Reagh. Marie MacCarthy Reagh was descended from a branch of that family which had settled at Toulouse in the late seventeenth century.

## CLOGHPHILIP CASTLE

There is little left of Cloghphilip Castle which was originally built in the thirteenth century by the Barrett family. The MacCarthys of Muskerry took over the building in 1488 and rebuilt a section of it a hundred years later. The castle, located near Blarney, Co. Cork, was damaged during the Cromwellian wars and although it was returned to the MacCarthys at the Resoration, it was not repaired.

## CLOGHROE CASTLE

Cloghroe Castle was the centre of power for the MacCarthys of Muskerry until the construction of nearby Blarney Castle in 1446. Cloghroe was built in the late thirteenth century by the de Guines family and later was inhabited by the Lombards. The MacCarthys ousted the latter family in the mid-fourteenth century and retained control of the castle until it was destroyed during the wars of the mid-seventeenth century. Cloghroe House was built nearby in the early eighteenth century by the MacCarthys, who had managed to retain their lands in the area. A later house now stands on the site.

CORMAC'S CHAPEL, CASHEL (See page 14)

COURTBRACK CASTLE

Only part of the curtain walls remain of this castle which is located near Blarney, Co. Cork. A branch of the MacCarthy family lived in the building from the late sixteenth century until the property was confiscated in 1641. The Courtbrack MacCarthys were descended from Donogh MacCarthy na Mona (who died in 1605) and were known as the "Masters of Mona".

CUL-NA-LONG CASTLE

This castle was probably built in the late sixteenth century by the Tadhg Ruadh na Scairte branch of the MacCarthys. It was held by them until the Cromwellian wars when the castle was confiscated. After 1660 it was returned to the clan who were not destined to hold it for long. After 1690 Cul-na-long passed to the Bernard family. The remains of the building can still be seen near Durrus in west Cork.

CURRAGH CASTLE

The MacDonogh MacCarthys of Duhallow took over this castle in the early sixteenth century from the MacAuliffes who were its original owners. It was the principal castle for the MacCarthys of Duhallow until the mid-seventeenth century when it was bought by Sir. Philip Perceval. There are now no remains left of this building-which was sited near Kanturk in north west Cork.

## DERRYLEAMLEARY CASTLE

A branch of the MacCarthy Reagh lived in this small castle which is located near Ballineen in west Cork. Like so many MacCarthy castles, Derryleamleary was confiscated in the 1640s but was restored twenty years later on the return of the monarchy. It does not appear to have been inhabited after the Restoration and was lost to the MacCarthy Reagh family after the events of 1690. The building was used for a time in the nineteenth century and is still in fairly good condition.

## DOWNEEN CASTLE

The location of this MacCarthy castle on the sea cliffs near Rosscarbery in west Cork has not helped its preservation. Part of the building fell into the sea in a cliff fall which has now isolated the remainder of the fortress on a large rock. Downeen belonged to the MacCarthy Reagh and was possibly built about 1500. In 1602 it was captured by an English force after the Battle of Kinsale and later in that century was owned by the Freke family.

## DOWNYNE CASTLE

Downyne Castle, built near Millstreet, Co. Cork, was held by the MacCarthys of Drishane in the sixteenth and early seventeenth centuries. By about 1650 the castle appears to have been in ruins and there is now no trace of the building.

## DRISHANE CASTLE

This fine building is still in good condition and stands proudly beside later additions to the property at Millstreet in Co. Cork. Drishane was probably begun by Dermot Mor MacCarthy, the brother of another important castle builder, Cormac Laidir MacCarthy. The castle was finished in about 1450 and was inhabited by the

MacCarthys until its confiscation under Cromwell. The loyalty of the Earl of Clancarty to the crown resulted in the return of most of the MacCarthy lands after 1660, including Drishane. However, the castle was again confiscated after 1690 and eventually passed to the Wallis family who built the nearby large house which was later used as a school.

## DROMSICANE CASTLE

Parts of the curtain wall and towers are the only remains of this castle near Millstreet, Co. Cork. It was probably built originally by the O'Keeffes but had passed to the MacDonogh MacCarthys of Duhallow by the early seventeenth century. In 1645 the castle was visited by the Papal Nuncio, Rinnuccini, en route to the Confederation of Kilkenny. The MacDonogh MacCarthys had lost control of Dromsicane by the end of the seventeenth century and the property subsequently passed to Sir Nicholas Chinnery.

## DUNDAREIRK CASTLE

The early history of this castle is unclear but a branch of the MacCarthys were in occupation of the building in the late sixteenth century. It was held by the clan until forfeited by Dermot MacCarthy in the 1640s. Dundareirk was probably not inhabited after that time and only a portion of the walls still remain. It is located near Macroom, to the west of Cork city.

## GARRYCLOYNE CASTLE

Garrycloyne was built near the MacCarthy stronghold of Blarney in the sixteenth century, probably about 1535. The MacCarthys themselves occupied it for a time but after the late sixteenth century it was inhabited by the Galway and Sarsfield families. It was confiscated from the Sarsfields in 1692 and subsequently passed through several owners. The castle, which has now disappeared, was probably not inhabited after the early nineteenth century when a large house was built nearby.

KANTURK CASTLE (See page 42)

KILBRITTAIN CASTLE (See page 19)

KILCOE CASTLE

Kilcoe Castle stands in a beautiful site near Ballydehob in west Cork. It was constructed by the Clan Dermot branch of the MacCarthy Reagh and the soundness of its design was proved by the difficulties encountered by the English forces who tried to take the castle after the Battle of Kinsale. Kilcoe finally surrendered in 1603 after a long siege. The building is still in very good condition.

KILGOBBIN CASTLE

The castle of Kilgobbin, near Ballinadee, Co. Cork, was a stronghold of the MacCarthy Reagh who constructed the building in the fifteenth century. The MacCarthys retained control of the area until the mid-seventeenth century when the castle was confiscated during the Cromwellian period. The MacCarthy Reagh clan do not seem to have regained the castle after that date and the property finally passed to the Palmer family who built an adjoining house in the nineteenth century. The castle is now in ruins.

KILMEEDY CASTLE

Kilmeedy Castle was originally built to defend a route through the territory controlled by the MacCarthys of Drishane, a branch of the MacCarthys of Muskerry. It was probably constructed by Dermot MacCarthy (brother of Cormac Laidir MacCarthy) and his son Tadhg in the mid-fifteenth century and is still in fairly good condition. Kilmeedy was held by the Drishane MacCarthys until the Cromwellian confiscations and later was returned to the family in 1660. The castle was lost after 1690 although the MacCarthys seem to have had some claims to it in the early eighteenth century.

## LISSANOURE CASTLE

Lissanoure Castle was an eighteenth century mansion which incorporated an older castle. It was built at Killagan, Co. Antrim by George Macartney who was a prominant diplomat and colonial governor. In the mid-nineteenth century the house was remodelled, but was badly damaged by an accidental explosion during the alterations and was thereafter left to ruin.

## LOHORT CASTLE

The castle of Lohort, near Cecilstown in north west Cork, is still occupied and is in good condition. The MacDonogh MacCarthys of Kanturk held Lohort from the late sixteenth century until the Cromwellian wars. In 1650 the castle was badly damaged following a siege, but was subsequently repaired. The MacCarthys may have held the castle after the Restoration of the monarchy in 1660 but by the eighteenth century the property was owned by the Perceval family (later Earls of Egmont).

## MACROOM CASTLE (See page 39)

## MASHNAGLASS CASTLE

This is one of the later castles built by the MacCarthys of Muskerry and is located between Coachford and Macroom to the west of Cork city. It was constructed in the late sixteenth century and was occupied mainly by the MacSwineys who were soldiers to the MacCarthys. The property was confiscated in 1641 but was restored to the MacCarthys after 1660. The Earl of Clancarty held Mashanaglass until it was lost after the Williamite wars. The castle is now in ruins.

## MONTEEN CASTLE

The Castle of Monteen, near Ballinascarty in Co. Cork was associated with the MacCarthys in the sixteenth and seventeenth centuries. It was probably built in the sixteenth century, but suffered damage in 1600 when it was burnt by the English forces during the tense period surrounding the revolt of O'Neill and O'Donnell. The MacCarthys remained in the area but by the late seventeenth century no longer controlled Monteen. The building is now in poor condition.

## MOURNE ABBEY AND CASTLE

Mourne Abbey, near Mallow, Co. Cork, was founded by the Knights Templar in 1199 and from the early fourteenth century was occupied by the Knights Hospitaller. After the Reformation the Abbey was granted to Teige MacCarthy. In 1520 an important battle occurred near the Abbey and its defensive castle when Cormac Og MacCarthy defeated the Fitzgeralds. MacCarthys were associated with the site for many years and the head of that branch was known as the "Master of Mourne". The ruins of the Abbey and Castle can still be seen.

## MUCKROSS FRIARY (See page 23)

## ROSS CASTLE

Ross Castle occupies a magnificent site on the lake shore just outside Killarney. It was built in the sixteenth century by the O'Donoghue Mor clan and was held by them until the late sixteenth century. After the Desmond Rebellion the O'Donoghues lost control of Ross Castle which then fell into the hands of the Earl of Clancare, Donal MacCarthy Mor. The MacCarthys did not own Ross Castle for long and by 1600 it was held by Sir Nicholas Browne. It was subsequently taken by Cromwell and later had a military barracks attached. It is now in the process of being restored.

## SRUGRENA ABBEY

This property is located near Cahirciveen in Co. Kerry. It was associated with the descendants of the MacCarthy Mor.

## TIMOLEAGUE CASTLE

There was probably a fortress at Timoleague, in west Cork, from the thirteenth century but the ruins of the present castle are of a later date. David de Barry built a castle there in the early thirteenth century and subsequently the Barry family submitted to the MacCarthy Reagh as overlords. The building was burnt during the Desmond Rebellion and Florence MacCarthy Reagh took possession of the site for a time, but the Barrys succeeded in regaining and rebuilding the castle. In the mid-seventeenth century a MacCarthy married into the Barry family. The MacCarthy Reagh claimed the castle as overlords until the end of the seventeenth century when the loss of the Jacobite cause resulted in the loss of MacCarthy power.

## TOGHER CASTLE

The MacCarthy Downey branch of the MacCarthy clan built this fine fortress in the sixteenth century. It is situated in west Cork, near Dunmanway, and was probably on the site of an earlier castle. The MacCarthy Downeys occupied the building until 1641 and Togher soon had a reputation for hospitality and culture. The castle was not regained by the MacCarthy Downeys after its 1641 confiscation and it subsequently passed to the Hoare family.

## MAJOR MacCARTHY LANDOWNERS, 1878

Macartney, George, Reps. of, Lisanore Castle, Ballymoney,
Co. Antrim, 12,532 acres in Co. Antrim; 276 acres in
Co. Londonderry; 310 acres in Co. Meath.

Macartney, John William Ellison, M.P., J.P., The Palace, Clogher;
Mountjoy Grange, Co. Tyrone, 625 acres in Co. Antrim, 506
acres in Co. Armagh.

MacCarthy, Alexander, Cork, 1,015 acres in Co. Cork and 2,979
acres in Co. Kerry.

MacCarthy, Alexander, Liscreagh, 3,832 acres in Co. Cork.

MacCarthy, Daniel, J.P., Headfort, Killarney, Co. Kerry, 2,203
acres in Co. Kerry.

MacCarthy, Daniel, Stugreana, Cahirciveen, Co. Kerry, 1,033
acres in Co. Kerry.

MacCarthy, Denis, Leeson Park, Dublin; Rathroe, Millstreet,
Co. Cork, 2,175 acres in Co. Cork.

MacCarthy, F. Daniel, J.P., Glencurragh, Skibbereen, Co. Cork.
1,032 acres in Co. Cork.

MacCarthy, Mrs. Helena, Harold's Cross, Dublin, 888 acres in
Co. Sligo.

MacCarthy, John, Grattan's Hill, Cork, 145 acres in Co Cork.

MacCarthy, Justin, Cork, 805 acres in Co. Kilkenny.

MacCartie, Justin, J.P., Carrignavar, Co. Cork, 3,435 acres in
Co. Cork.

MacCartie, Richard, Australia, 768 acres in Co. Cork.

## DISTRIBUTION SUMMARY OF MacCARTHY LANDS, 1878

| | |
|---|---|
| Co. Antrim | 13,157 acres |
| Co. Armagh | 506 |
| Co. Cork | 12,402 |
| Co. Kerry | 6,215 |
| Co. Kilkenny | 805 |
| Co. Londonderry | 276 |
| Co. Meath | 310 |
| Co. Sligo | 888 |

Total acres owned in Ireland: 34,559

Ross Castle

# A SHORT LIST OF MacCARTHY BIOGRAPHY

Macartney, C., late eighteenth century - early nineteenth century, actor and Author. Provincial actor in England.

Macartney, Carlile Aylmer, b.1895 , University Professor. Born in Kent, educated Winchester and Cambridge. Fellow of All Souls College, Oxford 1936-1965. Professor of International Relations, Edinburgh University.

Macartney, George, c.1660-1730, Soldier. Served with British regiments in Flanders and Spain between 1706 and 1710. Fled to Holland following a controversial duel in 1712, later surrendered and was found guilty as an accessory (1716). Restored to rank, made Lieutenant-General.

Macartney, George, (First Earl), 1737-1806, British Diplomat. Born at Lissancore, Co. Antrim. Served as diplomat in Russia (1764), Ireland (1769-1772), Caribee Islands, Madras, and Cape Colony (1796-1798). First British ambassador to Peking.

Macartney, George, (Sir), 1867-1945, British Diplomat. Educated in England and France. Served as diplomat in India and China 1888-1918. Was Consul General in China 1910-1918.

Macartney, Hussey Burgh, 1799-1894, Australian Clergyman. Born in Dublin, ordained in Church of England 1823. Served in Ireland until 1847, then emigrated to Australia. Served in Melbourne area, became Dean of Melbourne 1852.

Macartney, John Arthur, 1834-1917, Australian Pastoralist and Horseman. Born in Ireland, emigrated to Australia in 1848. Became successful sheep farmer and horseman in Queensland and Northern Territory.

Macartney, Mervyn Edmund, 1853-1932, British Architect. Born in Armagh. Surveyor to Dean and Chapter of St. Paul's Cathedral, London, 1906-1930. Played an important role in the preservation of St. Paul's.

Macartney, Samuel Halliday, (Sir), 1833-1906, British Doctor and Diplomat. On medical staff in Crimea (1855) and at Indian mutiny (1859). Served in China (1860-1875). Secretary to Chinese legation in London 1877-1906.

Macartney, William, eighteenth century, Author. Minister of Old Kilpatrick. Author of "Treatise of Cicero de Officiis".

Macartney, William Macleod, b.1912, Church of Scotland Minister and Author. Educated Scotland and Switzerland. Missionary in Africa 1938-1945, then Minister in Scotland. Author of "Dr. Aggrey" and "The Church and the Underdog".

MacCarthaigh, Christian, twelfth century, Abbot. Abbot of St. Jakob's Monastery, Regensburg, Bavaria, c.1140.

MacCarthy, Bartholomew, 1843-1904, Scholar. Born in Co. Cork and educated in Fermoy and Rome. Ordained Roman Catholic priest. German and Celtic scholar, noted for research on Stowe Missal (seventh century manuscript) and early Christian works.

MacCarthy, Charles, d.1665, Soldier. Son of first Earl of Clancarty whom he pre-deceased. Served in France and Low Countries. Died in naval battle between Duke of York and the Dutch in June 1665. Buried in Westminster Abbey.

MacCarthy, Charles, (Sir), c.1760-1824, Soldier and Colonial Governor. Also known as Charles MacCarthy Lyragh. Born in France, served in Irish Regiments in French army and (after French Revolution) in English army. Served in West Indies. Governor of Sierra Leone 1812-1824. Killed in battle with Ashantees.

MacCarthy, Charles J.F., b.1912 , Local Historian. Accountant by profession. Noted local historian in Cork and author of "Regional Defence: A Nation in Arms" (1944) and "Early Medieval Cork" (1969). Published numerous articles on many aspects of Cork history, particularly on St. Finbar and on medieval Cork. Involved in library and national monuments committees.

MacCarthy, Charles Justin, (Sir), 1811-1864, Colonial Diplomat. Lived in Ceylon where held posts of Auditor General (1847), Colonial Secretary (1851) and Governor (1860-1864). Was classical scholar and linguist. Knighted 1857.

MacCarthy, Cormac, seventeenth century, Soldier. Son of Felim of Glenachroim branch of MacCarthy Reagh. After confiscation of father's estates(1691)went to France and served in military there. Known as "Charles of Lorraine".

MacCarthy, Cormac Laidir, d.1494, See page 13

MacCarthy, Daniel, 1807-1884, Antiquarian. Born in London. Published "The Life and Letters of Florence MacCarthy Reagh" in 1867 and other works on the MacCarthy family.

MacCarthy, Daniel, 1823-1881, Teacher, Professor,and Bishop. Born in Kenmare, Co. Kerry. Educated at Maynooth where later taught rhetoric, scripture and Hebrew. VicePresident of Maynooth 1872-1878. Bishop of Kerry and Aghadoe 1878-1881. Author of religious works.

MacCarthy, Denis, eighteenth century, Merchant in France. Belonged to Clan Dermod branch of MacCarthy Reagh. Went to France after defeat of King James II. In Bordeaux established a mercantile house, "MacCarthy Freres", which operated for over one hundred years. Admitted to French nobility in 1756.

MacCarthy, Denis Florence, 1817-1882, See page 41

MacCarthy, Desmond, (Sir), 1878-1952, Writer and Critic. British. Author of "The Court Theatre" and "Leslie Stephen". Editor of "Letters of the Earl of Oxford and Asquith to a Friend" (1933).

MacCarthy, Eugene, d.1801, Soldier. Born in Co. Kerry. Served in Irish Regiment in France. Belonged to French expeditionary force in American War of Independence. After French Revolution served in Irish Brigade of English army. Died in West Indies of fever.

MacCarthy Reagh, Florence, c.1562-c.1640,
See page 21

MacCarthy, Florence, 1761-1810, Bishop. Born in Macroom, Co. Cork. Educated in Rome. Vicar General of Cork and Bishop of Antinae 1803.

MacCarthy, Florence MacTaidhg, eighteenth century, Sailor. Belonged to branch of MacCarthy Reagh which settled in Saintonge, France, in early eighteenth century. Served in French naval service until after the French Revolution, when emigrated to New Orleans in the United States.

MacCarthy, Hamilton Thomas, 1847-1939, Canadian Sculptor. Noted Canadian sculptor. Designed Boer War memorials for several Canadian cities, including Ottawa, Halifax and Quebec. Created Champlain monument in St. John, New Brunswick and J.A. Macdonald statue in Toronto, Ontario.

MacCarthy, Hamilton Wright, 1810-1882, Sculptor and Poet. Exhibited sculpture at Royal Academy, London, between 1838 and 1867. Died in London.

MacCarthy, John (Jacques), 1785-1835, Soldier and Publisher. Born in Nantes, France. Served in French army under Napoleon, including action at the Battle of Waterloo. Became publisher in Paris and later served in War Office. Was one of the founders of the Geographical Society of France and wrote several geographical works.

MacCarthy, John, 1815-1894, Bishop. Born in Fermoy, Co. Cork. Ordained as Roman Catholic priest in 1842. Served in Co. Cork. Bishop of Cloyne 1874-1894.

MacCarthy, John Baptist, 1765-1802, Ex-priest, Royalist/Brigander in France. Born in Co. Clare. Educated at

Nantes where became Roman Catholic priest. Later left church and entered business in Nantes. Experienced financial problems and was accused of organising a band of brigands to retrieve his fortune. Motives may have been political as he was a Royalist. Executed 1802.

MacCarthy, John Bernard, b.1888 , Author. Lived in Co. Cork. Author and Playwright. Works included "Crusaders", "Fine Feathers" and "Covert".

MacCarthy, John George, 1829-1892,
See page 29

MacCarthy, Justin, (Viscount Mountcashel), d.1694,
See page 16

MacCarthy, Justin, (Count), 1744-1812,
See page 25

MacCarthy, Nicholas Tuite, 1769-1833, Jesuit Preacher. Born in Dublin, son of Count Justin MacCarthy. Went to Toulouse with family in 1773. Studied in Paris. Ordained 1814 and joined Jesuits 1820. Renowned preacher, known as "Abbe de Levignac".

MacCarthy, Oscar, b.1815 , Railway promoter, Author. Born in France and settled in Algeria. Planned railway network for Algeria and wrote geographical works.

MacCarthy, Robert, J. 1769, titular 5th Earl of Clancarty. Son of Donogh, 4th Earl of Clancarty. Joined British navy. Was governor of Newfoundland 1733-1735. Failed to recover his father's forfeited estates. Settled in France 1741 and promoted Stuart cause.

MacCarthy, Robert Joseph, (Count), 1770-1827, Soldier and Politician. Born in Toulouse, son of Count Justin MacCarthy. Was monarchist so left France at Revolution and joined the Army of Princes. Returned to France 1814, served in cavalry and on war council. Elected deputy 1815-1820.

MacCarthy, Thaddeus, (Blessed), 1456-1492,'Bishop'. Probably belonged to the MacCarthy Reagh. Nominated to see of Ross and to see of Cork and Cloyne (Co. Cork). Both nominations opposed by other factions. Renowned for his piety. Died in Ivrea, Italy.

MacCarthy, Welbore, 1841-1925, Bishop. Belonged to Durrus branch of MacCarthys. Educated at Trinity College Dublin. Ordained to the Anglican ministry in 1867. Served in India, was Archdeacon of Calcutta 1892. Was Bishop of Grantham, England, 1905-1918.

MacCartie, Frederick Fitzgerald, 1851-1916, Doctor, Soldier. Belonged to Carrignavar branch of MacCarthys. Educated at Trinity College Dublin. Entered Indian Medical Service 1877. Served Afghan War 1878-1880. In 1898 was created Companion of the Empire of India.

McCartee, Divie Bethune, 1820-1900, Presbyterian Medical Missionary. Born in Philadelphia, United States of America. Became medical doctor at University of Pennsylvania in 1840. Missionary in China 1843-1872 and served in U.S. consular offices. Professor of Law and Science, Imperial University at Tokyo 1872-1877. Later was diplomat and missionary executive.

McCarthy, Adolf Charles, b.1922 , British Diplomat. Educated at London University. Served in Royal Navy 1942-1946 and then in Ministry of Agriculture, Fisheries and Food (1939-1964) and Ministry of Overseas Development t1946-1966). In diplomatic service from 1966 in Pretoria, Wellington, Stuttgart and Freiburg.

McCarthy, Alan, b.1938 , Businessman. Educated in Dublin and at Stanford University. Businessman and executive with Coras Trachtala (Irish Export Board).

McCarthy, Charles, 1873-1921, Political Scientist, Publicist. Born in Massachusetts, U.S.A. Director and organiser of first official reference library and bill drafting bureau in the U.S. for the use of legislators. Author of "The Wisconsin Idea" (1912).

McCarthy, Charles, b.1924, Academic. Educated in Cork, University College Dublin and Kings Inns. Professor of Industrial Relations at Trinity College Dublin and involved in many organisations. Professional board member, principally in state and semi-state companies.

McCarthy, Charles E., 1902-1979, University Official. Born in New York. Vice-president of St. John's University, Brooklyn. Company director.

McCarthy, D'Alton, 1836-1989, Canadian Lawyer and Politician. Born in Co. Dublin. Emigrated to Canada in 1847. Called to Bar of Upper Canada 1858. Was member of Parliament 1876-1898. Supported Conservatives until 1893. President of Imperial Federation League. Led opposition to the use of French language outside of the province of Quebec.

McCarthy, Donal John, b.1922 , British Diplomat. Served in Royal Navy 1942-1946. Entered Foreign Office in 1946, served in Jedda, Kuwait, Ottawa, Aden and at the United Nations. Ambassador to United Arab Emirates 1973-1977.

McCarthy, Eugene John, b.1916 , U.S. Senator, Writer. Educated at University of Minnesota. Teacher 1935-1940. In Military Intelligence for War Department 1940-1948. Representative in Congress for Minnesota 1949-1958. U.S. Senator 1959-1970 (Independent). Author of political works.

McCarthy, Frederick David, b.1905 , Australian Anthropologist. Educated in Sydney, Australia. Curator and field researcher in Australia, Indonesia, Malaya,and Arnhem Land. Author of

"Australia's Aborigines" and numerous scientific papers and monographs.

McCarthy, J. Thomas, b.1937 , U.S. Professor of Law. Educated in Detroit, U.S.A. Held law posts in California. Visiting professor at University College Dublin, 1975.

McCarthy, James Joseph, 1817-1882,
See page 37

McCarthy, John, b.1938 , Businessman. Educated in Ireland. Developed business network of garages, hotels, etc. in Ireland.

McCarthy, John F., 1862-1893, Member of Parliament. Provision merchant in Tipperary. Represented mid-division of Tipperary as Member of Parliament 1892.

McCarthy, Joseph Raymond, 1908-1957, U.S. Senator. Born in Wisconsin. Represented Wisconsin in U.S. Senate 1947-1957. Accused many individuals of subversive (Communist) activities - known as McCarthyism 1950-1954. Censured by Senate 1954.

McCarthy, Joseph Weston, 1915-1980, Editor and Writer. Born in Massachussetts, U.S.A. Newspaper reporter 1936-1939. Military service 1941-1945. On editorial staff of "Cosmopolitan" 1946-1948 and then freelance. Contributed articles to many publications. Author of "The Remarkable Kennedys" (1960) and "Ireland" (1964).

McCarthy, Justin, 1830-1912,
See page 33

McCarthy, Justin Huntly, 1861-1936, Writer, Historian and Member of Parliament. Son of Justin McCarthy, writer and politician (1830-1912). Was Member of Parliament from 1884 to 1892. Wrote plays, novels and historical works, including "The Candidate", "The Illustrious O'Hagan" and "Outline of Irish History".

McCarthy, Leighton Goldie, 1869-1952, Canadian Diplomat and Businessman. Born in Ontario, Canada. Lawyer and businessman. Canadian minister to the U.S. 1941-1943. Ambassador to U.S. 1943 to 1944.

McCarthy, Lillah, 1875-1960, English Actress and Manager. Noted English actress. Roles included Gloria in "You Never Can Tell" and Viola in "Twelfth Night". Assumed management of the Little Theatre (1911), the Kingsway (1912 and 1919) and the Savoy (1912).

McCarthy, Mary, b.1912 , Writer American theatre critic, editor, lecturer and broadcaster. Author of "The Company She Keeps" (1942) and "The Group" (1963).

McCarthy, Mary Frances, b.1916 , Educator. Joined Sisters of Notre Dame de Namur. Teacher in Philadelphia, Washington and Boston.

McCarthy, Niall, b.1945, Television Producer, Director. Educated at University College Dublin. Producer/director of programmes, documentaries etc. for R.T.E. (Irish television).

McCarthy, Niall St. John, b.1925, Judge. Educated at University College Dublin. Called to Bar 1946 and had large practice. Created Supreme Court judge in 1982.

McCarthy, Nicholas Melvyn, b.1938, British Diplomat. Educated at London University. Joined British diplomatic service in 1961 and served in Saigon, Tokyo, Brussels, Dakar, Osaka and at the Foreign and Commonwealth Office. Received O.B.E. in 1983.

McCarthy, Patrick Peter, b.1919 , Solicitor. Educated in Liverpool. Practiced as solicitor 1942-1974. Chairman of Industrial Tribunals in Liverpool (1974-1987) and London (1987-).

McCarthy, Peter, b.1934, Businessman. Educated in Massachusetts, U.S.A. Senior Financial Analyst in U.S. Company Director and Vice-President in Ireland.

McCarthy, Sean, b.1937 , Politician, Physician. Educated at University College Dublin. Qualified as surgeon, worked in Mater Hospital, Dublin and at University College Dublin. Involved in local and national government. Was T.D. (Member of Parliament) for Tipperary South 1981.

McCarthy, Sean P., b.1933 , Engineer, Local Government Official. Educated at University College Cork. Engineer with local authorities in several Irish counties. County Manager 1982-.

McCarthy, Thaddeus Pearcey, b.1907, Judge. Born and educated in New Zealand. Practiced as barrister and solicitor until 1957. Appointed to Supreme Court 1957. Judge of Court of Appeal (New Zealand) 1963-1976, President 1973-1976. Served on many Royal Commissions and other committees. Chairman of New Zealand Press Council 1978-.

McCarthy, Thomas, b.1954 , Poet. Educated University College Cork. Poet and editor. Publications include "The Non Aligned Story Teller" and "The Sorrow Garden".

McCarthy, William Edward John. (Baron), b.1925. Industrial Relations Expert, Academic. Educated at Oxford. On numerous committees of inquiry and investigation since 1968, especially in connection with industrial relations. Opposition spokesman on employment 1980-. Author of works on industrial matters, such as 'closed shop', shop stewards, collective bargaining, trade unions etc. In 1975 was created Baron McCarthy of Headington, Life Peer.

McCarthy, William T., 1885-1970s. Judge. Born in Massachusetts. Admitted to Bar 1908, practiced in Boston. Appointed judge of U.S. District of Massachusetts in 1949.

McCartie, Patrick Leo, b.1925, Bishop. Educated in England. Became Roman Catholic priest 1949. Involved in parish work, education, administration and served on committees etc. Auxiliary Bishop of Birmingham and Titular Bishop of Elmham 1977.

McCartney, Gordon Arthur, b.1937 , Solicitor, Local Government Official. Educated at Wrexham, England. Admitted as solicitor 1959. Solicitor to several borough councils from 1959. Secretary of Association of District Councils 1981-.

McCartney, Hugh, b.1920 , Member of Parliament. Educated in Glasgow. Worked in several industries. Active in Labour Party. Involved in local and national government. Labour Member of Parliament 1970-1987 for Scottish constituencies.

McCartney, Ian, b.1951, Member of Parliament. Son of Hugh McCartney, Labour M.P. Labour Party Organiser 1973-1987. Involved in local government. Labour M.P. 1987-.

McCartney, James Paul, b.1942 , Musician, Composer. Born in Liverpool. Belonged to highly successful 'Beatles' group 1960-1970. Formed 'Wings' 1971. Composer and performer of numerous songs. Appeared in films, on television etc.

McCartney, Washington, 1812-1856, Lawyer, Solicitor. Born in Pennsylvania. Practiced as lawyer and jurist. Was noted mathematician and educator in Pennsylvania.

McCarty, Charles Justin, d. c.1790, Canadian Preacher. Born in Ireland. Emigrated to United States where became follower of evangelist George Whitefield. Went to Canada 1788 and became controversial preacher there. Arrested 1790 charged with disturbing the peace etc. and was deported to New York.

McCarty, Denis, d.1820, Australian Farmer. Born in Ireland. Convicted and sent to Australia in 1800. Pardoned 1810. Farmed near Hobart Town, Van Diemen's Land (Tasmania) and eventually owned considerable land and property. Explored south west coast. Charges of smuggling (1814) and assault (1817) overturned.

McCarty, Frederick Briggs, b.1926 , Electrical Engineer. Educated in Texas. Held electrical engineering appointments in California. Company director.

McCarty, Lois Reeves, b.1907, Businesswoman. Owner and operator of major women's clothing business in California, U.S.

McCarty, Richard, d.1781, Officer, Lawyer, Fur Trader. Born in Connecticut. In Militia 1757-1760. Moved to Montreal, Canada by 1765. Commissioned as Barrister 1768. After 1770 was fur trader in Michigan/Illinois area. Later involved in rebel activities.

# BIBLIOGRAPHY

## Books, etc.

Barrington, T.J., "Discovering Kerry: Its History, Heritage and Topography", Dublin: Blackwater, 1976.

Burke, Sir Bernard, "Burke's Peerage and Baronetage" and "Burke's Landed Gentry of Ireland", London: Burke's Peerage, 1904-1970.

Butler, William,F.T., "Gleanings from Irish History", London: Longmans, Green, 1925.

Hayes, Richard, "Biographical Dictionary of Irishmen in France", Dublin: M.H. Gill, 1949.

Healy, James N., "The Castles of Co. Cork", Cork: Mercier, 1988.

Holohan, Renagh, "The Irish Chateaux: In Search of Descendants of the Wild Geese", Dublin: Lilliput, 1989.

Hussey de Burgh, U.H., "The Landowners of Ireland", Dublin: Hodges, Foster and Figgis, 1878.

MacCarthy, Daniel, "A Historical Pedigree of the MacCarthys of Gleannacroim", Exeter: n.p., n.d. (c.1880).

McCarthy, S.T., "A MacCarthy Miscellany", Dundalk: Dundalgan, 1928.

McCarthy, S.T., "The MacCarthys of Munster", Dundalk: Dundalgan, 1922

O'Hart, John, "Irish Pedigrees", New York: Murphy and McCarthy, 1923.

O'Murchadha, Diarmuid, "Family Names of Co. Cork", Dun Laoghaire: Glendale, 1985.

Sheehy, Jeanne, "J.J. McCarthy and the Gothic Revival in Ireland", Belfast: Ulster Architectural Heritage Society, 1977.

Weir, Hugh W. L., "The MacCarthys, Lords of Desmond", Shannon: Shannon Development, 1981.

## Journals

Butler, W.F., "The Pedigree and Succession of the House of MacCarthy Mor", Journal of the Royal Society of Antiquaries of Ireland, Ser.6, Vol.XI, 1921, pp.32-48.

Collins, J.T., "A McCarthy Miscellany", Journal of the Cork Historical and Archaeological Society, Vol.LIII, 1948, pp.95-103.

Collins, J.T., "Some McCarthys of Blarney and Ballea", Journal of the Cork Historical and Archaeological Society, Vol.LIX, 1954, pp.1-10, 82-88; Vol.LX, 1955, pp.1-5, 75-79.

J.P.D., "Necrology: Most Rev. John MacCarthy D.D., Lord Bishop of Cloyne ...", Journal of the Cork Historical and Archaeological Society, Ser.I, Vol.III, 1894, pp.14-16.

MacCarthy, R. MacF., "The MacFinnin MacCarthys of Ardtully", Journal of the Cork Historical and Archaeological Society, Ser.II, Vol.II, 1896, pp.210-214.

McCarthy, W., "Note on Some Nautical MacCarthies", Irish Sword, Vol.V, No.19, 1961, pp.120-121.

## Journals containing MacCarthy material

Capuchin Annual, 1948

Journal of the Cork Historical and Archaeological Society, 1892, 1894, 1896, 1897, 1901, 1904, 1906, 1907, 1908, 1909, 1917, 1928, 1947, 1951, 1961, 1965, 1966, 1968, 1983, 1984, 1985.

Irish Builder, 1882, 1886, 1888, 1889, 1891, 1899, 1901, 1904.

Irish Ecclesiastical Record, 1865, 1902, 1950.

Irish Sword, 1963, 1965.

Kerry Archaeological Magazine, 1908, 1909-1917, 1920.

Journal of the Kilkenny and South-East of Ireland Archaeological Society, 1857, 1858-1866.

Journal of the Royal Historical and Archaeological Association
  of Ireland, 1883
Journal of the Royal Society of Antiquaries of Ireland,
  1906, 1907, 1921.
University Magazine, 1879
Journal of the Waterford and South-East of Ireland
  Archaeological Society, 1896

## MacCARTHY SURNAME VARIATIONS

Macartney

MacCarthaigh

MacCarthy

MacCartie

McCartee

McCarthaigh

McCarthy

McCartie

McCartney

McCarty

Cormac Mac Carthy's crozier

## Other Publications by Ballinakella Press include

*Houses of Clare*, Hugh Weir
*Ireland – A Thousand Kings*, edited Hugh Weir
*O'Brien: People and Places*, Hugh Weir
*O'Malley: People and Places*, Sheila Mulloy (co-publication)
*Burke: People and Places*, Eamon de Burca (co-publication)
. *Ireland: Sketches of Some Southern Counties*, Holmes (facsimile)
Lloyd's *Tour of Clare* (facsimile)
Henry's *Upper Lough Erne* (facsimile)
*Trapa – A Spanish Irish Story in Spanish and English*,
        H. Weir and T. Porcell
*Máire Rua, Lady of Leamaneh*, Máire Mac Neill